THE GREATEST PLAYER

Kevin L. Michel

"Those who approach life like a child playing a game, moving and pushing pieces, possess the power of kings." – Heraclitus

MICHEL BOOKS

Published by MICHEL BOOKS LLC.
www.KevinMichel.com
Copyright © Kevin L. Michel, 2017, 2020
All rights reserved

No part of this book may be transmitted or replicated in any form by any means, be that electronic, mechanical, photocopying, recording, or any format, on any device, without the prior written permission of the publisher.

Set in 9 / 11 / 12 pt Minion Pro
Product Dimensions : 5.25 x 0.41 x 8 inches
Printed by Kindle Direct Publishing
Cover design and interior layout by MICHEL BOOKS

Contact: Kevinlmichel@Gmail.com

ISBN-10 : 1733127100
ISBN-13 : 978-1733127103

BOOKS BY KEVIN L. MICHEL

Moving Through Parallel Worlds To Achieve Your Dreams
Your World Shifts: Transform Your Life Instantaneously
Alpha Dominance in Tennis: A Letter to Aloysius
Virtue of The Gods: A Letter To Aloysius
Subconscious Mind Wealth
Subconscious Mind Power

CONTENTS

Introduction	7
Are You There?	10
The Nature of the Game	12
This Document	18
PART 0001	21
PART 0010	33
PART 0011	51
PART 0100	65
PART 0101	79
PART 0110	95
PART 0111	109
PART 1000	125
GOAT	144

Introduction

Tuesday, July 14th 2314, and the singularity is a distant memory. For now is a time of social excellence, some inequity, a time of abundance, and broad global prosperity. An abundance catalyzed, realized, by exponential growth in computing technology. We remain on a path of continued human evolution, yet in a world that has advanced beyond all recognition.

I can see the similarities in behavior and personality between human beings at the likely time of your reading this, and humans at the time of this writing. Technology advanced, and with it came an integration of this technology with human cognition. The hardware, mostly, is the organic human brain. The software, partly, is digital. Genetic engineering, nanotechnology, neural links, all creating a human cognitive system that is a hybrid of organic and machine elements. Humans today, are in part machines, and our cognition includes the ability to process and run digital programming.

It is fair to say that we have advanced and evolved. Still, we remain human. We are whatever being human has always been. We are mortal, arguably – we are functionally immortal. 423 people died last year, some by chance, most by choice. Still, so much of consciousness remains after life, that the definition of death is at best, a consensus.

The connection between technology and the human brain is outstanding, imperfect, and intriguing. We can now upload information and programming to the brain in a way that is instantaneous to the outside observer, but what is very curious is that for the individual experiencing and then processing the upload, the process feels sequential, arduous, and time consuming. The process feels hardly any different than it did for a student sitting in a 20th century classroom, interacting with a digital tutor and a script. The perception of an upload of information, for the individual, is still one of effortful cognition. Transferring information, digitally, to the human brain, is imperfect due to the perception of extended transfer time.

An interesting analogy is the way human beings, historically, have perceived and experienced the passage of time. That is, although the initial theory of relativity, and the unified theory which enhanced it, showed that all things happened, happen, and will happen, simultaneously – a single moment, all encompassing, a proof of the underlying instantaneous multi-tiered simulation – human perception, human intuition, human cognition, led to a perception of time passage occurring sequentially – the brain, by its nature, creates the illusion of sequence.

That is the point – time occurs as an illusion in your world, because you are *not* in your world. Your apparent world of electrons that are real only in terms of their charge and relation to each other, yet nothing physical, albeit, the very definition of physical. That is the point. You are not in this world. You are not of this world. Your body, resides, in 2314. Your mind, is engaged in a computer simulation, modeled on the human experience, and set in the time of you reading this. Right now, you are interacting with digital programming. Right now, you experience the illusion of time and the perception of cognitive effort.

Introduction

The experience for those of us observing you, is almost instantaneous. You are in, and then you are out. We do then edit and replay the footage of your experience over extended periods of time, for research and entertainment purposes. You typically partake in the screening, promotion, and distribution. Life happens, fast, but your experiences always take on a new meaning when you sit in the audience.

You, are meant to read this. The purpose of you reading this shall become clear. What is certain, is that, whatever you have decided shall be your purpose in this life – what you are now reading shall get you there faster, and with greater poise.

The game of life you have chosen, willingly. You chose to play that game, and I propose that you could choose, consciously, to play this game. To accept the premise, the mythology, philosophy, simulation hypothesis – accept that Nick Bostrom was right. Accept the premise, that your physical body resides in the year 2314. Accept that you are in a simulation right now. You are a simulated version, of a part, of your 2314 self. Start there.

Yet, this is not just a simulation. It is much more. It is a hybrid experience that is novel and cutting edge in the 24th century. This experience is best described as a hybrid game. Hybrid, because it is many things. It is a game, a sport, an experiment, reality entertainment, live performance, many things. The entire simulation is simply called "You," and it is placed in our genre of "game/sport."

Are You There?

This book is not for everyone. Seriously. You need not spend the time. Many will read this book and find great insight therein, but, it is written primarily, for one person. That person may be you, and, maybe you know if it is you, but maybe you do not. I certainly do not know exactly what form the avatar of the greatest player shall take. In any case, this is a great point to turn back. If you are considering reading this book, and have read this far, then this is a great point to put the book down and move on to a book with more words and a flashier cover, and I assume smoother formatting. If you have already committed to reading this book, then this is a great point to save yourself the time, and give it to someone else without much explanation, or leave it on the bus, or train, or plane. Time is your most precious resource, seemingly.

Alternatively, this is an ideal point to become fully immersed. This is an ideal point to face reality, or at least, simulated reality.

Reality? The reality, is that no one book can make you fulfill your greatness. But, you can decide, you can intend, for a book to have a profound impact in helping you to achieve that greatness. In the pursuit of greatness, our simulations have shown that for much of human history, the power of suggestion, and the power of grit, are often the most potent and readily available cognitive enhancements – Duckworth was right. To this day, the power and plasticity of the neuron is still unrivaled. The human brain, and its quantum processing power, even to this day, remains valuable, and astounding.

Introduction

The reality, you can decide and you can intend, for a grain of sand to have a profound impact in helping you to achieve your greatness. Your greatness emerges from a power, and a structure, that is within you. And it is in that spirit, that I humbly ask you to intend that this book will have a profound, powerful, positive impact on your performance.

For it is *not* about a book, and it is not about an author – it is about you. It is about you deciding that right now is the time for you to take it to the next level and make your move to greatness. If you cannot make that decision, then there is no point to all this. There is no point in reading, there is no point in assessing, there is no point in wasting the next hour of your time, there is no point in reading any other book. The sand shall pass through the hourglass, the illusion of time shall persist, the moment gone, the opportunity wasted.

The Nature of the Game

Approximately 10 million players have been immersed into this multidimensional simulation "game," each somewhat in their own world but influencing players and activities across many worlds. There is an audience. You typically join the audience upon completion of your play – because your play, which is your life, for those of us viewing in 2314, is complete, in a matter of seconds. Your play is then viewed over two weeks, in this case the viewing is in the year 2314 and you typically enter the game again after a few weeks off when the process is repeated. You do occasionally skip a round of play when you feel a greater need for mental recovery. The audience includes both players and non-players. The audience is currently over 12 billion people.

The game has many objectives, but the ultimate goal, is for 2314 humanity to study and be entertained by the players who are most able to have a significant positive impact on the worlds that they find themselves in. Positive economic, political and social advancement of the simulated human species in each world.

It is an amazing experiment and it is an unbelievable show, an unrivaled game and sport – a truly unique experience for those involved. Those who play possess phenomenal talent and skill, and they are a life changing experience to behold. That is the point. Their play makes us all better. Their play inspires. Their play changes the world in 2314, because their play changes the world of the simulation. These players are so good that they are not allowed to bring their full intellectual prowess into the simulation. Their memories of who they are in the year 2314, are heavily suppressed. Their consciousness in the simulation being only a part of their wisdom and awareness prior to entering the game.

It is the case that some knowledge can be brought into the game and some knowledge cannot be brought into the game. Your awareness in the game is between 3 and 4 percent of your awareness outside the game. The exact percentage varies for each player, but for elite players, it is within that 3 to 4 percent range. Once you plug into the game, the intense realism of the simulation and the ability of our technology to suppress areas of your prefrontal cortex - areas of reasoning, lead to your simulated "You" being just that small percentage of your true self. There is confusion at first, there is pain, there is emptiness, but the mind very quickly begins to latch on to and accept the reality it is presented with.

Several parts of the brain of the player are actually rewired by the experience, but this is mostly in areas of the motor cortex, some prefrontal cortical regions, and is no different than the effect of any type of learning. But it is the restriction of consciousness to only 3 to 4 percent that is so intriguing. This is part of the challenge of the game. This is why the game is so hard and played by relatively so few. Some would say that being the partial self in the game is like comparing the concept of the human soul to the human body. The soul being the full "You" whilst the body is just an avatar that has the essence of the soul and can be tested on the physical plane. That is one way to describe it, but maybe this is just an analogy.

As noted the suppression of mental faculties and the percentage of the full self brought into the game varies for each player. Some players are able to bring more of their full self into the simulation. Some players are able to bring more awareness into the simulation. It is a skill that separates players, and the top 1000 players in the simulation are known for increasing their awareness, as each game progresses.

The top 1000 players are known for also increasing the awareness of other players as the game progresses, which because of the nature of the algorithm and the objectives of the game, serves to improve the ranking of the player who impacted other major players. In the game, to improve others, directly or indirectly, is to improve the self. To share awareness of the game, is to increase one's power.

All very interesting. Here you find yourself now, being provided with this information. Probably, this gets to you in the second half of the twenty first century, but I cannot be certain. Probably this information shall reach you in the form of bio-synced literature, audio text, printed, digital, or some other book format. Yet, I have not written a book.

Although I am creating this content, now, in the year 2314 – you are reading a translation. I have written some computer code, and added it to the simulation, to the game. Code, that in effect, says "communicate this idea to 10 million specific players in 10 million separate worlds, in the language of each player." 10 million specific players in 10 million separate worlds. Upon exposure to this idea, the player becomes different, and each world becomes different. The right words, have the power to change a player.

Introduction

So then, this content shall reach 10 million players. It is a work that is handed from player to player. For some, it is ludicrous. For others, it is genius. Each player reads it differently. Each player responds to it differently. Some players stopped reading several passages ago. Some players shall encourage others to read it.

Each player who reads it, learns to dominate the game, in their world. Each player who reads it, learns to fulfill their potential. Each player who reads it learns to transform their world. All this serves to improve the research outcome from this simulation. All this serves to improve the entertainment value, for the many spectators. All this raises the quality of play. All this, I deem as necessary. I trust that the process from the encoding of this idea, to the communication of this idea in the format that you are now receiving it, leaves little lost in translation.

We have gotten this far, I shall share with you something else. It is something, slightly, sinister.

You must know, that I do not have approval from the administrators of the simulation to pass on to you this content. I do not have permission from the administrators of this simulation to write and insert this code into your program. This is my will, and it shall be done. And who am I? I am you. If you think through all that I have said, you will realize that I am suggesting that "You," actually refers to 10 million different people. I will not explain this, as to do so requires the explanation of parallel realities, the many-worlds interpretation of quantum physics, and how each human avatar is moving through parallel worlds in every moment of existence.

I cannot explain any of this without positively affecting the advance of science in all worlds, which would then alter far too many variables in this simulation simultaneously, making it significantly more difficult and expensive to track the impact of the individual player on the simulation – which is one of our core research objectives. Confounding, it would be, and it is very expensive and time consuming to handle in post. The simulation, the sport, the research, the game, as serious and fun as it is, does have a profit motive. Some things stayed the same.

Having written the code, and assuming that this idea reaches you in the format of a book, let me speculate further about precisely how you get access to this information. The copyright holder and listed author in your world is intended to be the relatively unknown, Kevin L. Michel. In about 7% of the currently simulated worlds, events unfolded such that Michel, would have written a book, in the early 21st century about parallel universes, and many worlds, and moving through parallel worlds to achieve your dreams, and in other worlds this is the first book to bear his name. Michel, is the person I have chosen, you have chosen, as cover for the release of this information into the game. He has accepted that responsibility and he holds the copyright and author credit. Who are you? You are me. Who am I? I am you. The answer to both questions is the same, and only the forthcoming answer is relevant. Who are you? You are the greatest player. The greatest of all time. You are ranked number 1 in the world.

Introduction

In your world. Does it feel like you are that great? That is what 3 to 4 percent of your consciousness feels like. 3.9% is your average in prior games. You are the greatest player, and you wrote the unapproved code that created this document. As a player of the game, and to have written this code which ultimately produced this document is not a cheat move. Not a cheat, but more similar to a foul in typical sport. It is like the opponent is making an advance to your goal and you shoulder-checked them.

What you have done here is probably a penalty violation - I am sorry to inform you, however, you are such an inspiration and ambassador for the game that the officials are not likely to call you on this, and your fellow players just shrug and move on. Watching you create this code is like watching (in 12% of simulated worlds) Michael Jordan commit a traveling violation - the performance is such a work of art, such magic, and the player's reputation so great, that the officials no longer seem to even observe that a violation may or may not have occurred - such is part of your greatness. I have digressed. For I wish I could tell you that you are all good, but that is not the case. You are not all good - you are great.

This move here, this code, this document, is considered part of the greater game and all part of play, and you have done this many times before, and your opponents have done it in different forms as well. It is just a game, albeit hybrid. Some fans will hiss, some fans may boo; all gathered now, they're watching, You.

This Document

Then what is this book that ultimately you created? This book is designed to increase your own awareness of the mindset, methods, and philosophy that you have used to win this game consistently. This book, because of the code you created, has taken on the format as the "Notes of the Greatest Player."

This book is read only by the greatest player - a designation that is specific to you, but in parallel realities is actually shared by many. This document is new programming, it is your code, and you should approach it as such. Over 10 million copies will be sold in what you perceive as your world, yet the number 2 player will not embrace this knowledge, even though he receives it – that is why he is number 2.

Another player who reads it may well be the greatest player in another dimension – a player with a success record as great as your own, but the moment he is exposed to this book, his reality splits. To understand this is to understand the unfolding beyond the event horizon of a black hole – in that, our species comes to understand all this, sooner than expected, before 2314, but, you, have decided not to explain this here.

That is your choice.
You are pressed for time.
You have code to complete.
Done.

You have been exposed to this program.
You will expose others, actively.
You will transform your self.
You will transform this simulation.
You will transform your world.
Those exposed will transform *their selves*.
They will transform their simulation.
They will transform their world.
Your work is done.

Read the notes of the greatest player, and trust and internalize.
Read frequently, like a meditation, like a mantra.
Memorize what you can.
Live, what you can.
Live the life, of the greatest player.
Win.
Again.

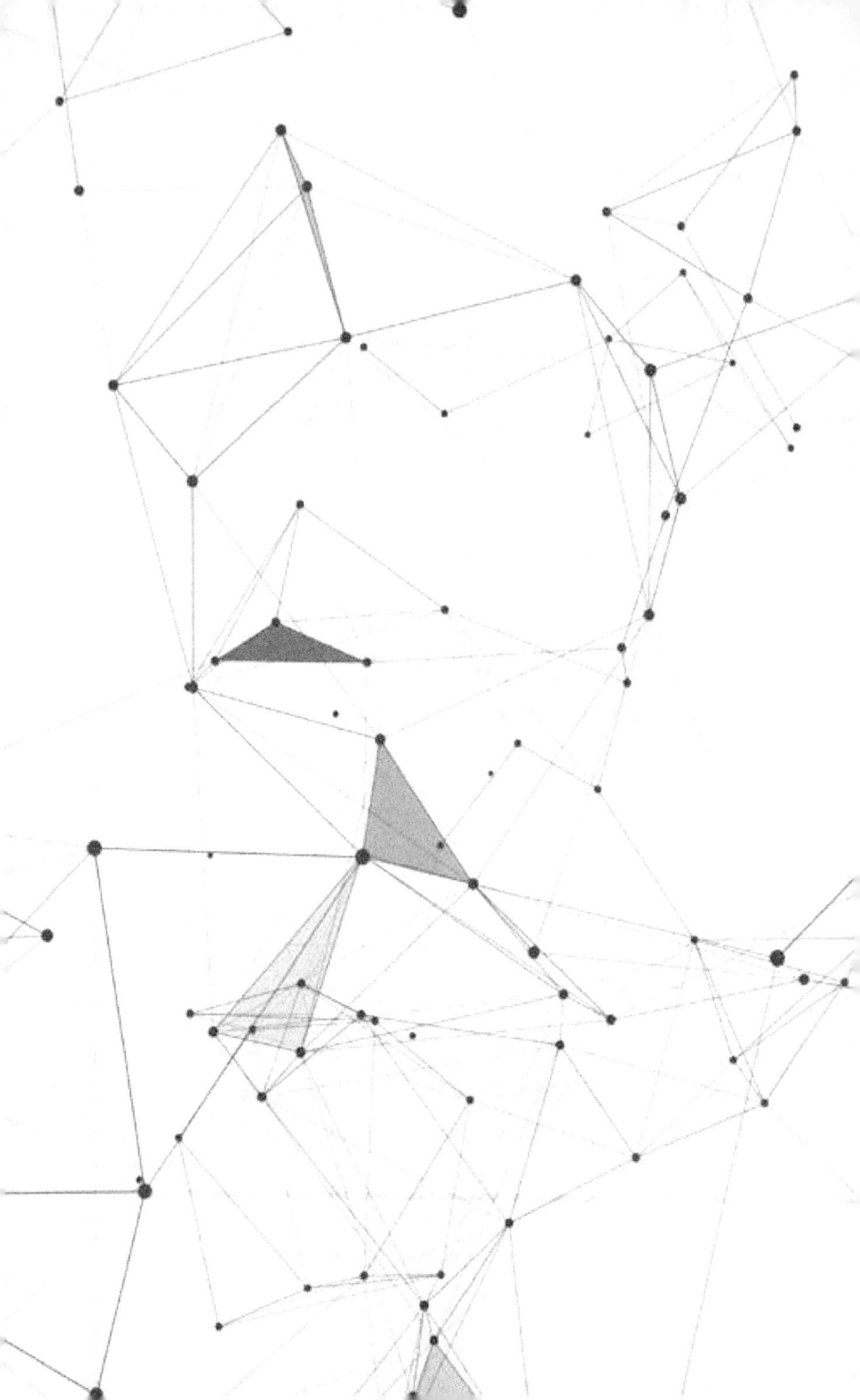

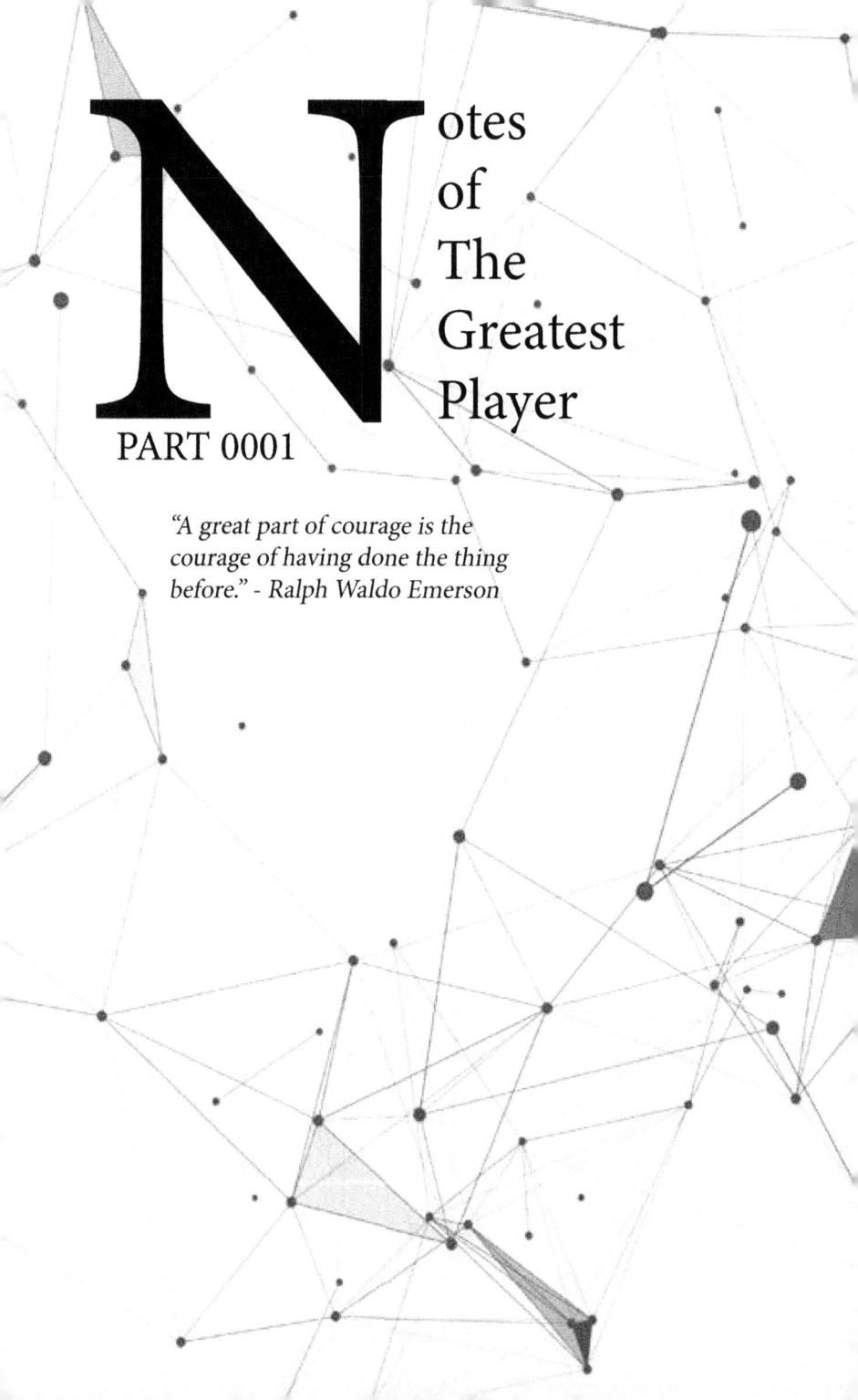

Notes of The Greatest Player

PART 0001

"A great part of courage is the courage of having done the thing before." - Ralph Waldo Emerson

Ineo

Every game begins with the suppression of memory.

Every game begins with forgetting.

The greatest player forgets that he is so great.

This is called birth.

This is called life.

This is an essential feature in the game, and makes it all so immersive.

The greatest player has a powerful skill.

A skill that is characteristic of the top 1000 players.

He retains high levels of memory and increasing awareness.

He remembers, and becomes aware of his nature as a player, and specifically, as the greatest player.

Exoculo

Many of the top players are exposed to their true nature, yet they doubt the truth.

They lack awareness of this game.

They lack awareness of this ruse.

They seldom raise their gaze, their play is boxed, in fact, obtuse.

Impressive they are still, but they just won't have the range.

Their promise unfulfilled, blind to their power, they can't see their use.

Umbra

The greatest player sees the illusion more clearly each day.

Increasingly he sees the games people play.

When at times he is wise, well, that is the source.

He knows that illusion is part of the course.

Laurus

The game is won through the creation and implementation of a global strategy.

The creation and implementation of a system, a product, a campaign, an event, a manner of existing, that positively shifts the advance of the human species.

A positive shift that increases the rate of social, economic and political progress in the human species.

The strategy is based on an activity, but the activity is not as obviously powerful as one may imagine.

Is it being a brilliant mother, a brother, a friend?
Is it running a successful business or being a great academic?

Is it modeling a rise from poverty to prosperity?

Is it overcoming physical disability?

Is it just exceeding expectations habitually, arithmetically, exponentially?

It is not clear, and for you, it has been different every time.

All I can say, is that the activity is, pivotal.

IMMORTALIS

The ultimate end of the game is human immortality within your lifetime.

It is out of reach now, but that is how the game is won, and that is how the game has always been won.

Ironically, the point where immortality is achieved is the point where the game ends.

Immortality is not what you directly pursue.

At times, the greatest player has contempt and disdain for the very idea of immortality.

But his actions, show that he does pursue it, indirectly.

Immortality, and achievement of the win, is done by a slight increase in the arc of human progress.

Best said, is that human immortality is achieved through a butterfly effect, and you are the butterfly.

Recrepo

When you observe the world; when you see what is unfolding in the news.

When you see success, when you see tragedy; all these things are your game.

All these things are your world.

You influence the world of your game; you shape the world of your game.

You create the world of your game.

It is a game of influence.

Your micro actions affect macro actions.

Your example reverberates throughout the field of play.

Your words are heard and words alter the day.

"What!?" You chant cause now you're on your way.

All have gathered . . . it's time to save the day.

Epistola

There are many reasons why you are the greatest player.

One of the reasons, is that in every game you play, you find a way to get key messages to your avatar self.

A message to the portion of your consciousness that is engaged in play.

The key messages: first, that this is a game; second, a message of key strategies, behaviors, and traits, that have led to you becoming the greatest player.

This document, is that message to you.

In 2314, where you entered the game, you wrote all this.

These are your words, your mantra, your meditation, your message to you, the greatest player.

Locus

The greatest player knows that productive study, deliberate practice, rehearsal and preparation time, are all highly valuable.

When he is engaged in productive work, he dares not stop.

He does not over-train and is mindful of his health and wellness, but he dares not stop for other reasons.

He stays in the zone.

He lives in the zone.

He builds habits in the zone.

He knows the important work,

That is his first work of the day.

It is the last thing he rehearses, at the end of the day.

First, foremost, last, and avoiding cessation.

That is key to producing his momentum.

Avatar

The greatest player trains, physically.

He is indistinguishable from a professional athlete.

Life is the sport, life is the game.

He is in the gym, 3 days a week, 4 days a week, 5 days a week.

There is no escaping this.

Every biological function is affected by the physical conditioning of your avatar.

Your intellectual prowess, your leadership potential, your sustained mental drive and motivation, the emotional, moral and financial support you receive from others.

All are affected by the conditioning of your avatar self.

The greatest player knows that physical conditioning is a lifelong pursuit, that is always required, so he learns to love it.

You develop a passion for the intensity of training.

When the body feels weak, when the pressure of exercise is too great, when the body says it can do no more, you remind yourself, that you and the body are not the same.

You remind yourself that you are not this avatar.

In a manner of speaking, you are the soul.

You are the player - the greatest player.

You transcend this simulation.

Processus

The greatest player's productive efforts are repeatable.

He is quickly into the rhythm of productive work.

He gets there effortlessly, easily and without fanfare.

He sets himself up, well, allowing for minimum delay in the commencement of his work.

His process repeats and it evolves.

He chooses a special place, reserved only for his most important work.

He protects this place.

It is the physical zone that creates the mental zone.

He builds the habits.

Notes of The Greatest Player

PART 0010

"The self is best measured against the self." - Kevin L Michel

Grandis

The greatest player is a closer.

You crave the big opportunity, and you seize it.

You crave the pivotal moment and you seize it.

You identify the big opportunity, and you seize it.

You are not surprised to be a major contender.

You are not surprised to find yourself in a moment where the quality of your play matters.

You are not surprised to find yourself, having to make daring and big moves in the game.

You are not surprised, to find that you must raise your intensity, aggression and productivity, in many critical moments.

The greatest player knows that there are significant challenges up ahead, and he expects them.

He is comfortable and focused in those key moments.

He is not surprised by the bigness of the moment.

How could he be surprised by bigness?

He himself is huge.

He does not choke.

He is ready.

He is prepared, and has been preparing for years.

He knows that because of his greatness, those big moments are inevitable.

Doge

The greatest player is an entertainer.

An entertainer of the minds at the pre-game level.

Billions watch.

Crowds are thrilled.

Tremendous ratings.

You are aware that it is all a stage.

You are aware that this is the field of play.

You are aware of the aesthetics.

You are aware of your environment.

You keep it interesting.

You keep it entertaining.

You put on a masterclass exhibition.

You embrace the narrative arc.

You are restrained, restricted and ridiculed, yet you show understanding and forgiveness, as you emerge stronger.

You are at times, selfless.

Part of the story is the hero's journey.

You overcome adversity.

You face off against certain death.

You win against the odds.

Like a beaten dog, you were.

Left for dead.

Guess who got up?

The greatest player.

Still bruised, you laugh.

You think;

"Wow!"

"Such story arc!"

"Very show!"

"So drama!"

"Much entertainment!"

Part 0010
Judit

The game began with the customization of your avatar.

Your avatar changes in most games, and you have great choice in its customization.

Indeed, selecting the avatar for play is a skill in and of itself, and as the greatest player you are very good at selection.

So what then?

When you face racism, sexism and discrimination?

What?

Do you realize that you selected those obstacles as part of your game?

Do you realize that you chose those elements?

Admittedly, with some restrictions, you customized those elements.

You decided that these were the battles that you would wage.

That those were unique, finely adjusted elements which you could use, to win.

You knew that certain attributes which seem like weaknesses, are actually components of your judo.

You shall leverage them to create power.

Certain elements that seem advantageous, are indeed advantageous.

You added those strong elements as a means of dominating your game, so, you must use them, responsibly.

After all, there are tradeoffs that come with those strengths.

There is complacency that can result from privilege.

You considered all this and you chose your avatar expertly.

Part 0010
Collusionem

It is not just your avatar that you customized, you also helped design several aspects of the game.

Many players make contributions to the design of the game, and such is an accepted practice.

However, because of your advanced ability to design code, you contributed more than most.

And most players thank you for it, because your code is always quite good.

But truth be told, you are an insider.

You grew up around other players of the game.

You grew up around designers of the game.

You played many test and practice versions of the game. There are many top players who are insiders, and you are one of them.

Just a fact; definitely a privilege; certainly carries the weight of expectation.

An insider.

Your parents were both players, and they were highly skilled.

They helped you to be great before you even entered elite competition.

This is part of the reason you became so great, so quickly.

Conmutatio

All players make prior alterations, to the world they shall find themselves in.

Certain elements, certain themes, some algorithms, each changed before one begins.

Each can take the risk of inputting certain code meant to give them a competitive advantage, but may risk point penalties by so doing.

But the hand of the player is always in part, the hand of the creator.

So how does it feel, knowing that you agreed to the elements of the game prior to entering?

Does it give you a sense of peace?

Knowing that you co-created, altered, selected, actively promoted, the game . . . does this give you a sense of power?

It should.

Knowing that all that you see is the result of your initial choice, and all that shall emerge henceforth shall be the result of your action.

That would.

All blame reserved for the self.

Very hard to be the victim when you are the creator.

The victim you are not.

You're the greatest player, you just forgot.

Haereo

There is so much sub-programming in the game.

One of the interesting bits is that other players receive subconscious prompts designed to get you to forget who you are.

They are, in a way, attempting to get you to doubt yourself, forget your genius and fail to realize your potential and greatness.

They are not consciously complicit in this.

They are not villains.

Some of them genuinely love your avatar and persona.

It is is just part of the central programming of the game, and it is one of the elements in the degree of difficulty that you agreed to when you started play.

Similarly, you, when you are not at your best, also become blind to the potential of others, and fail to see their full potential, contributions, and future capabilities.

You also bring others down, and weaken them, when you are not in full flow.

You blindfold them to their strengths, also in an unintentional manner.

You believe that you are just dealing with reality, and rightly so, for you deal only with the reality you see.

CELIARAI

I affect the whole.

I transform the whole.

Just as we look to the elite athlete for the peak of human achievement, the pre-game minds of the millions of other players, the billions of spectators, look to the greatest player for the peak of achievement in this simulation.

Many study the way the consciousness of the greatest player is able to take over an avatar, and step into a new world, and transform it through local action - through chain reaction.

That is what you do, and it is the reason why you play.

You show the world exactly how this is all done.

Regnum

Does the greatest player use energy to fulfill his purpose?

Does the work of the greatest player require effort?

Is their strain?

Is there the possibility of permanent obstacle?

There are all and many things the greatest player confronts.

All and many things.

Indeed, there is a certain fate to the greatest player's work.

There is a certain level of imperfect inevitability.

Inevitable in the sense that you have done this all before.

You have won before in more challenging circumstances.

You have won before at more challenging venues.

Many have said that for you, this venue is easy.

You are unable to remember the near disaster that occurred when the planet called Earth was simulated, and used as a venue.

A near disaster for you, in that, you nearly lost that game, such a close finish.

Yet your performance, in the mid to final stages of the Earth venue, is generally regarded as a classic performance – indeed a masterclass for greatness.

What a victory that was!

Indeed, the future design of a venue as challenging for you, as was Earth, is unlikely, and rule 23.4 forbidding the repetition of a player's most challenging venue (except in instances of a mid-game penalty violation, where the rules call for the current game to be paused and the venue imperceptibly changed to the most challenging venue of the offending player), shall ensure that Earth will never be simulated again.

Many have said that you are invincible in this format of the game.

When things are going well, and when things are not going well, you remind yourself that this is the easiest of venues – the easiest of planets.

PART 0010
MODESTIA

The greatest player has a certain swagger.

This is unavoidable.

Yes, he is humble.

His exterior appearance is one of humility; definitely.

Necessarily.

Much of his mindset embraces, shall we say, the concept of humility.

He is very humble.

He thinks he may be the most humble person ever, right?

So very humble and pious, yes?

Never breaks the rules, right?

Some of his confidence seeps out.

Not just confidence in himself, but confidence in others; confidence in the future of our species.

Because, you know.

You know of the inevitability.

You know of your power.

THE GREATEST PLAYER

You know that not only do you play at the highest level, but with patience and rapidity, you upgrade the highest level.

No one can beat the greatest player in this game.

Everyone just observe.

Take notes.

One time he said, "I wish the competition was better."

He may have been joking, or half-joking.

But seriously, notes.

You too.

Take notes on the instances of your greatness.

Take notes on how you managed to seize the day.

Take notes on how you overcome the next obstacle.

Take notes on how you transformed a situation and transformed yourself.

Write these notes every night, as you will need them all again, for there is an entire season of games to be played.

Fluxus

The greatest player takes time to recalibrate.

She recalibrates when faced with new conditions.

She recalibrates when faced with old conditions.

Fluid she is.

Completely wet.

She toasts: "To change!"

She pours champagne.

She fears not weather, for it's she who reigns.

Now watch her adjust to new terrain; "To new obstacles!" "To new features!" "To new pathways!"

To fight through pain.

She develops, new behaviors to achieve desired responses.

She knows that different responses shall arise from some of the same behaviors.

She knows that some of the same responses will arise from different behaviors.

She recalibrates, she knows, she flows.

She is completely immersed, all consumed, and even lost.

Terrain is new.

Each moment new.

Lessons remembered, pain is naught.

She is not just capable of a few things, so watch her adjust, adapt and learn new things.

She learns quickly and learns to learn more quickly.

Notes of The Greatest Player

PART 0011

"In this world, where the game is played with loaded dice, a man must have a temper of iron, with armor proof to the blows of fate, and weapons to make his way against men." – Arthur Schopenhauer

Animi Silienti

He can access his mind.

The unconscious.

The seedbed of behavior.

He meditates.

Daily.

Twice daily.

He plants ideas.

Thrice daily.

He sort of lives there.

A walking meditation.

That's where the flow happens.

That's where the magic is created.

That's where he creates his own powerful illusions.

The mind believes such unusual things.

He puts the mindset on himself, and then he gets the flow again.

Part 0011

He does not need to climb, for he is lifted.

In an instant he gains access.

He enters his subconscious.

He forgets the cause, but he trusts the process.

He puts the mindset on himself.

Visualizes to prepare.

He sees, to rehearse.

He has been there, he has done that.

Conlineare

Every moment is an answer to the question: "What would the greatest player do?"

An answer to the question, "What would you do?"

This is how the greatest player finds himself and becomes no longer lost in this illusion.

He finds himself because he seeks alignment with himself.

"How would the greatest player handle this situation?"

"How would the greatest player find the focus he needs right now?"

"How would the greatest player transform this situation?"

"What future situation will the greatest player face and how can he prepare now for its arrival?"

He asks the questions that lead to alignment.

"What would the greatest player do?"

He also thinks about what the avatar would do.

He is not the avatar.

The avatar is driven by habit, and greatly by dopamine, so he predicts in advance where the avatar is seeking to go.

Part 0011

He knows what it wants to do.

He builds the habits.

He uses the dopamine – cognitive judo.

He has some fun.

The avatar does not know that a path is being built.

Habits.

The greatest player's actions are focused on creating habits.

Every action builds a habit.

Every thought builds a pattern of thought.

He knows this.

The avatar takes the next logical step, but the greatest player has prepared a way for him.

Trajectoriam

The greatest player has missed an opportunity today. Sad!

So what!?

It is possible that this was a miss, but look at the year he has been having!

Look at his progress over the last 5 years, and his progress this decade.

Absent this, you can still view the trajectory of his game.

Look at the half-decade you are about to have.

Look at the progress you will make this decade.

Look at the potential of your game.

Do you think I am a normal player?

Do you think because I am behind on the score that I will fail?

You must not know much about theater.

Have a seat.

Part 0011

Have several seats.

Maybe you should not keep your head down?

You should be watching this.

Watching the long game.

The infinite game.

He is training, he is evolving; investing ahead of the curve.

Enriching stuff!

Variation

The greatest player has range; wiser he becomes, every day.

His knowledge is broad.

His knowledge is focused.

How does he do it?

Breadth and focus?

He is always learning.

Decades of improvement.

Decades in pursuit of excellence.

RIVALIS

The greatest player is a tremendous competitor.

He does not compete by destroying his opponent.

He competes by being better than his opponent.

As such, his only battle is with himself.

He battles with himself to be more focused.

He battles with himself to be more efficient in training.

He battles with himself to practice and prepare more thoroughly - more effectively.

With him, no one can compete, not in the long term.

Those who battle him face defeat, yet so much do they learn.

But destroy them, he does not; better, they become, ironically.

Thus even his enemies he gives a lot, all are improved by his proximity.

Forma

The greatest player operates with integrity.

He operates with proper form.

He does what he knows to be right.

He decides what is right in light of the fulfillment of purpose.

He seeks to win the right way, and sometimes he misses a point, the right way.

He seeks to win the right way, and the foundation he builds is stable.

His form is magnificent, in that it serves its function.

That is how he assesses form.

Form is that which is effective and sustainable.

Form is that which is effective and powerful.

Form, is that which allows him to win consistently with great margins.

VISUM

The greatest player has a vision.

The greatest player has a plan to implement his vision.

He is course correcting and adjusting, and always focused on the destination.

Importantly, he knows his purpose.

He knows what he is here to do.

It is well documented.

He meditates on it.

It guides his every action.

Adscensio

Each day you become more like the greatest player; more like who you truly are.

These words, part meditation and part prayer, align your avatar.

More purpose filled in each moment new, more rich as your day moves on.

Fuller, richer, reclaiming your you; yet long 'til the game is won.

Fabula

The greatest player knows when to pause, she knows when it is time to rest.

She knows when it is time to recreate, time to enjoy friendly and familial requests.

To dance in this theater, be nude at the beach, to play, drink and indulge.

Relaxation and effort - there is time for each, and she knows just how to judge.

Notes of The Greatest Player

PART 0100

"The self is the friend of a man who masters himself through the self, but for a man without self-mastery, the self is like an enemy at war."
– The Bhagavad Gita

Tardus

The greatest player takes time to understand her strengths.

She takes time to understand her areas of advantage.

Never satisfied, she continues to enhance those strengths.

Her strengths are what win her the game.

She can take a few steps backward, and then, she has loaded tremendous energy.

She can wait for things to align, she can play late, in perfect time.

She can move to a better position, then unleash a phenomenal weapon.

She knows the skills that makes her great; she knows when to use them, she knows when to wait.

Part 0100

Nox

The greatest player shall never concede in the pursuit of his purpose, for he shall never need to.

Even when it is dark; even when loss appears inevitable; even when he is down on the scoreboard; the greatest player believes; he believes he can win every point.

He battles for every point.

Not so much 'battles' but better stated, he 'pursues' every point, knowing that he can win and knowing that the current moment and the current point shall matter.

Those who seek to challenge him know that he is relentless, so they do not bother, or they exhaust and frustrate themselves.

Some would like to see him fail, so they can prove that hard, passionate, deliberate work yields scarce reward, yet such thinking is often folly, so they exhaust and frustrate themselves.

INFINITUM

The greatest player embraces the infinity of every moment of training, and he embraces the infinity of every moment of effort.

When the challenge is tough the greatest player believes that the challenge shall persist.

By so doing the greatest player does not hope for a break.

He does not hope that the training will soon be over, he does not hope that in a few moments the pain will be gone.

He embraces the pain, enjoys the pain, celebrates the pain.

By so doing the greatest player sets his mindset to one that is prepared to persist.

By so doing the greatest player is willing to train longer because he realizes that training and preparing is eternal.

The greatest player embraces the moment, he embraces the pain, he enjoys all of it – knowing that it shall never end.

By so doing, he makes the pain irrelevant.

By so doing, he ends the pain and achieves the training.

This is the mindset of the greatest player.

So then, what persists forever for the great player?

Part 0100

Study persists forever.

Practice persists forever.

Improvement persists forever.

Key productive work, persists forever.

The 20% that produces the 80%, persists forever.

He does not seek reprieve from these effortful areas.

The avatar goes onwards, and engages in these effortful tasks.

The habit is grooved, the avatar walks the path.

Paellucidus

The greatest player knows.

She knows that the challenge shall become more difficult, as each day passes.

She knows, that she must keep getting better, just to keep up, and to advance.

She knows that tomorrow will be more challenging than today.

Because tomorrow she will push herself harder, and further.

She must improve today, the next day, and improve even more on the following day.

Tomorrow she must be more focused.

Tomorrow more efficient.

Tomorrow quicker off the mark.

More organized, more lucid, more productive.

So today, she does all this, for growth is its own skill.

She practices the skill; she practices growth itself.

Evoco

The greatest player is calm, poised and relaxed in the face of threat.

She sweats but then towels her palms, she waivers not even for death.

Now still, it's the challenge that moves, familiarity is so hard to ignore.

So fluid she slides through its grooves, and recalls that she's done this before.

Responsio

It does not surprise the greatest player that others cannot see the future.

No surprise that others do not see his greatness until deep into the game.

Some sense it, but most resist it, downplay it, or think nothing of it.

There is a danger in this that the greatest player is alert to. The crowd's reactions affect the way that ordinary players play.

The ordinary player seems almost as if he is working to meet the expectation of the crowd, instead of being guided by an internal vision.

The greatest player does nothing of the sort.

The greatest player is aware that the conservative expectations of others is merely part of the game, so he is protected from it.

He finds his light and guidance and belief within himself.

Part 0100

He pulls to him people who believe in his potential; and he is cautious with the majority who do not yet believe.

He is not hostile to the majority, but he is cautious.

He is aware that they do not possess much foresight.

Who does possess much foresight?

Only the greatest player.

Although, even this is not entirely true, for the source of the greatest player's foresight is his ability through thought and action, to create the future.

SONITUS

The greatest player has clarity of intention; distraction he surely forsakes.

The noise won't divert his attention; there's purpose in each move he makes.

Not for long, can you be distracted.

Not for long can you be off course.

Eyes cautious to where they're attracted, on focus to channel your force.

Detrecto

The greatest player uses, practice, study and training; and she finds continual improvement, with no excuses and no explaining.

Aware that growth is the goal of every movement; growth is the nature of her work.

Growth is what is expected, a task she must not and does not shirk.

Exceeding that which was projected; nothing else can this Sim do.

That is how she makes the play, invests one point then moves up two.

Actum

Explanation is not a technique of the greatest player.

At least not verbally, as his actions have the power of speech.

The language is rolled up into the manner of his play.

This keeps him focused on right action.

This keeps him doing the work that is necessary for success.

He knows that it is real action which will bring him to fulfillment of purpose.

Surely, he can make his history seem more glorious by effective, targeted, oration, but he knows that his energies are best invested in progressive, sustained action.

Hodie

What a full day you have!

What a purpose filled and purposeful day you've had!

The answer to the question, "What did you do today?" is inevitable: "Today, you did a lot!"

Practice, play, planning, progress, persistence.

The greatest player ends the day having done much.

The greatest player ends the day having moved forward.

The greatest player ends the day having raised the base levels.

You have upped your game and you have upped *the* game.

This is why you play.

This is why your performance is viewed by so many minds, and by so many players.

This constant elevation is the reason you are the greatest player.

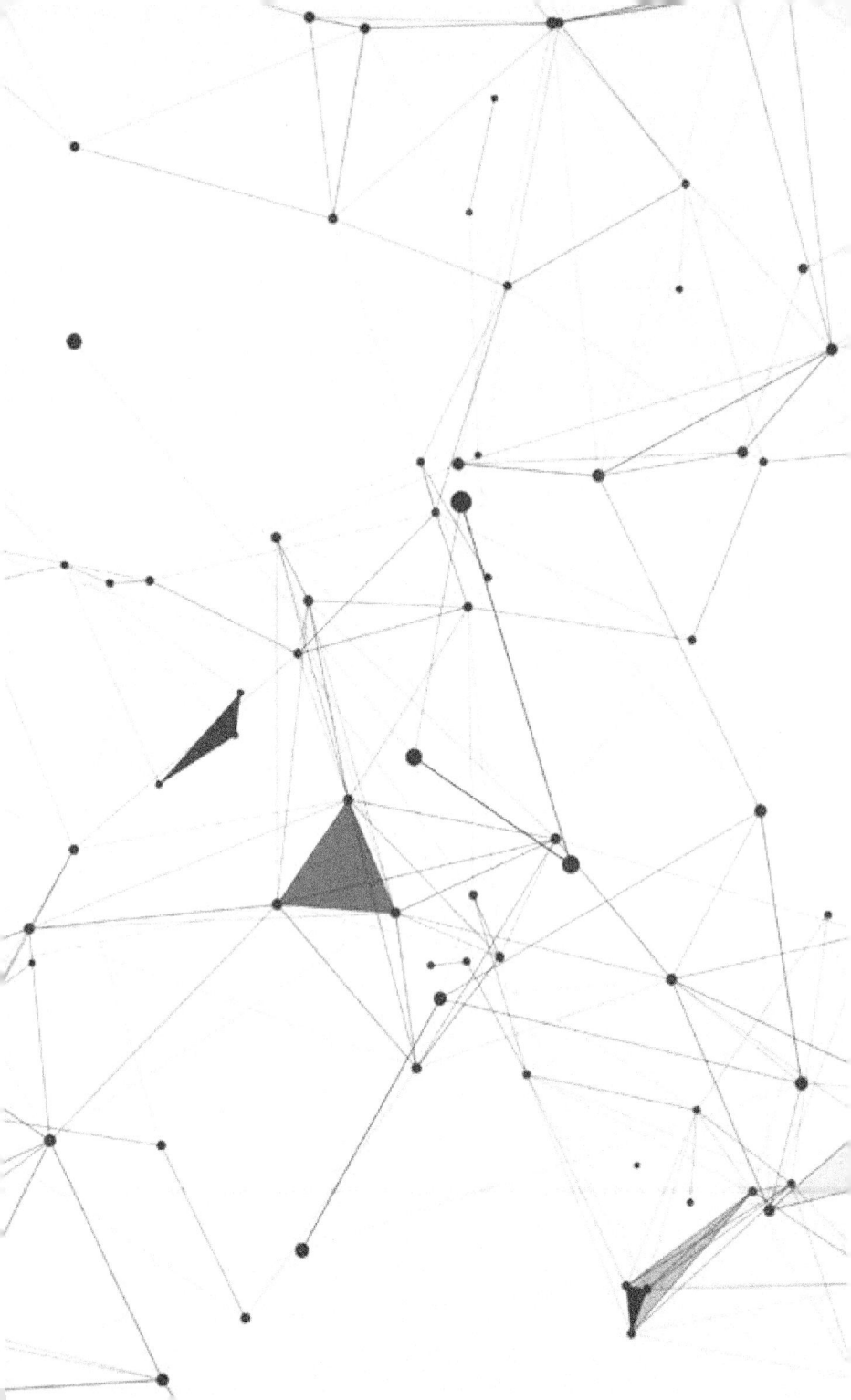

Notes of The Greatest Player

PART 0101

"Man suffers only because he takes seriously what the gods made for fun." - *Alan Watts*

OBSTINATUS

As the greatest player you are continually building and reinforcing effective habits.

You feed, and weave, and strengthen great habits.

Bit by bit, moment by moment, you strengthen and build upon greatness.

Bit by bit, and moment by moment, you build this victory.

Things happen more slowly in this world, the pace drags, it is harder to have the full impact of your force to seize the victory in an instant.

Strategy drags on, patience is needed.

You crave no respite, you dream of no unnecessary rest, you are entrenched in this moment.

Seizing and carving this moment.

Crafting and creating this moment.

Crafting, creating, and constructing this moment.

This world is slow and resistant, but you are unyielding amidst your great fluidity.

You are unflappable, defiant, unstoppable.

PART 0101

Nunc

Intense is the focus of the greatest player.

Intense, concentrated and conscientious.

In this moment you are, fully.

Possessed by this moment, engaged in this moment, fully in this moment.

Step by step, you advance, by making the most of the now.

By seizing the opportunity here.

The habit of maximizing the achievement in the now, gives you the confidence to lay out a plan of action, to imagine a path, to conceive a process, with the knowing that as you have done in every other game – you will execute one step at a time, as you move toward victory.

Conspicuum

The greatest player is able to step out of his own mind.

He can step into the mind of another, and then predict their actions, because he understands their perspective.

He can step off the stage, and sit in the audience, and enjoy the theater of the game.

He can provide himself with objective advice.

As he sits, he can see the separateness between the self and the avatar.

He can predict the movements of the avatar.

He is in this moment, yet one step ahead of himself.

Gradus

Speed is an essential component of his play.

The greatest player takes full advantage of speed.

He looks to get more done in less time.

He works in powerful bursts.

He knows that each moment builds on the next,
And that by getting more done in this moment, he gets more done in the next.

He builds the habit of getting more done in each moment.

Very fast he is.

Quick.

Faster than previously imagined.

Few other players have been this fast.

Few spectators have witnessed such speed.

Faster in each new game he plays.

He is learning in a way that fosters even greater speed.

The force comes not just from muscle, but from continually refining his technique.

His method is far from broken, yet he keeps fixing it.

What a madman!

Speed is a virtue to him.

Yes, style, and consistency and function are also virtues.

He does not sacrifice those things, yet he values speed.

He understands that the purpose of each action, is as an end, in and of itself, whilst simultaneously adding momentum to the next actions.

In a sense, each action has an explosive potential.

Each action has an effect, each action makes an impact, and each action explodes.

You should see it!

I must re-iterate because watching him live can lead to a false impression – that is, it looks like it is pure power and influence that leads to his speed, but the technical aspects of his actions are what generate the pace.

Anew

In an instant, the greatest player transforms himself.

He is born anew, or created differently, in an instant.

All that is required is a decision.

All that is required is an insight, and bam, his play is different.

He is different and the balance of the game is different.

To the spectator it seems discontinuous, and in a way, it is.

Yet he transforms so often that change is his greatest consistency.

I say he has hacked evolution, somehow he seized control of it, so he evolves continually.

There is much below the surface though; actually, it took him decades of work to learn to transform so instantaneously.

De Novo

Once, did the greatest player fail.

There was that one time.

And it was arrogance that caused it.

Overconfidence.

It is ironic, for you must wield great confidence to win, but confidence, overconfidence, one time, destroyed you.

It was very early on, when you first started playing the game.

You were already number one in the world.

You were already viewed as the very future of the game.

A young genius, a young maverick.

A string of great wins.

A top ranking.

Unrivaled.

Yet you lost.

Once.

You learned from it.

Part 0101

You are ever watchful now, because of it.

You know what arrogance looks like.

You know when pride cometh.

You know, to be cautious.

You remember.

You started to pay attention to the crowd.

You could hear them, specifically.

Their words began to matter, too much.

You began to think that their feedback was well intentioned.

You began to internalize their thoughts.

At training, a peculiar phenomenon began to affect you ... whereas normal players train harder when they are being watched, for the greatest player, it has always been a bit more complicated.

Simply, you started to train with less intensity when being watched.

You started to push yourself less hard when being watched.

You did not want them to see how engaged in training you were.

You did not want them to feel that you were odd for training so hard.

You did not want them to see that you were possessed; possessed by the need; possessed by the drive, to improve.

The need, the drive, to be better.

You would not even admit that you had a night of study ahead.

You would not even admit that you had many hours of research left to do.

You would not even admit that you had skill development that would take you all day, all week, all year.

You thought that being honest about this would cause you to not fit in; forgetting, you did, that the greatest player does not fit in.

You started to think that this intensity of effort would make you seem abnormal; forgetting, you did, that the greatest player is not normal.

You thought your concentrated effort and focus would make you seem crazy - forgetting, you did, that the greatest player is completely out of his mind.

That is why you are great.

That is why no one, to date, has been able to compete.

That is why, you lost, only once.

Perpetuus

Practice does not seem to stop, for you, the greatest player.

Training is ceaseless.

Every encounter, every moment, contains the opportunity for improvement.

This is the purpose of every encounter and every moment.

This is intertwined with the purpose of your existence.

This is intertwined with the purpose of the game.

Practice is that which heightens your ability to execute as you fulfill your broader purpose.

Practice is that which exponentially accelerates your advance to the end game.

Your mindset can be described as, a growth mindset.

Your mindset suggests an unlimited potential for growth.

You will be better, not just tomorrow, as this, for you, is inevitable - you will be better in the next moment, and the next.

You grow relentlessly.

Growth is your core programming.

Even in the midst of battle, you are rehearsing and evolving your gameplay.

You consider the move just prior and consider the practical improvement of future similar moves.

You are improving at this very moment.

You are improving skills that matter.

You are relentlessly improving.

Esus

The greatest player is a master of timing.

You, on occasion, will make a play earlier than is expected.

In other moments, the play is late and thus has a different effect.

A master of timing you are.

You draw out the time and you accelerate the time.

You use patience, and just as smoothly, you can force the play.

All is perfect, even the imperfections.

You see not the perfection.

Look now, if your head is down, it can only be through consumed, concentrated, and conscientious play.

Your mental faculties diluted not by frequent moves into the third person.

Yet always aware that this is a game, that this is the play.

You play, just this moment, on its merit, not yet stepping back.

From move to move, you are consumed.

Even still, the broader awareness is enmeshed in your being.

ADLUCINATIO

Many illusions and even delusions possess the mind of the greatest player.

These illusions and delusions serve you.

One such: You always believe that you can win.

With disregard to the direness of the current situation.

You believe that you can and will turn it around and you subsequently proceed to do exactly thus.

It is that illusion that makes so many of your victories possible.

It is that delusion that makes you so entertaining to watch.

Remember the debacle that was predicted during the Earth simulation – look how that ended.

It is delusion and illusion which created that win.

It is illusion and delusion that now fuels you.

Vanesco

He can disconnect like no other.

He can silence devices.

He can eliminate communication.

He can evade technology.

He can remove himself from the planet.

He does all this to remind himself of the silence.

The silence is within him, and sometimes he accepts a physical reminder.

Sometimes he stops to alter the environment, but then he is lost again, then he is immersed once more, then he reenters the zone.

He loads his power in silence.

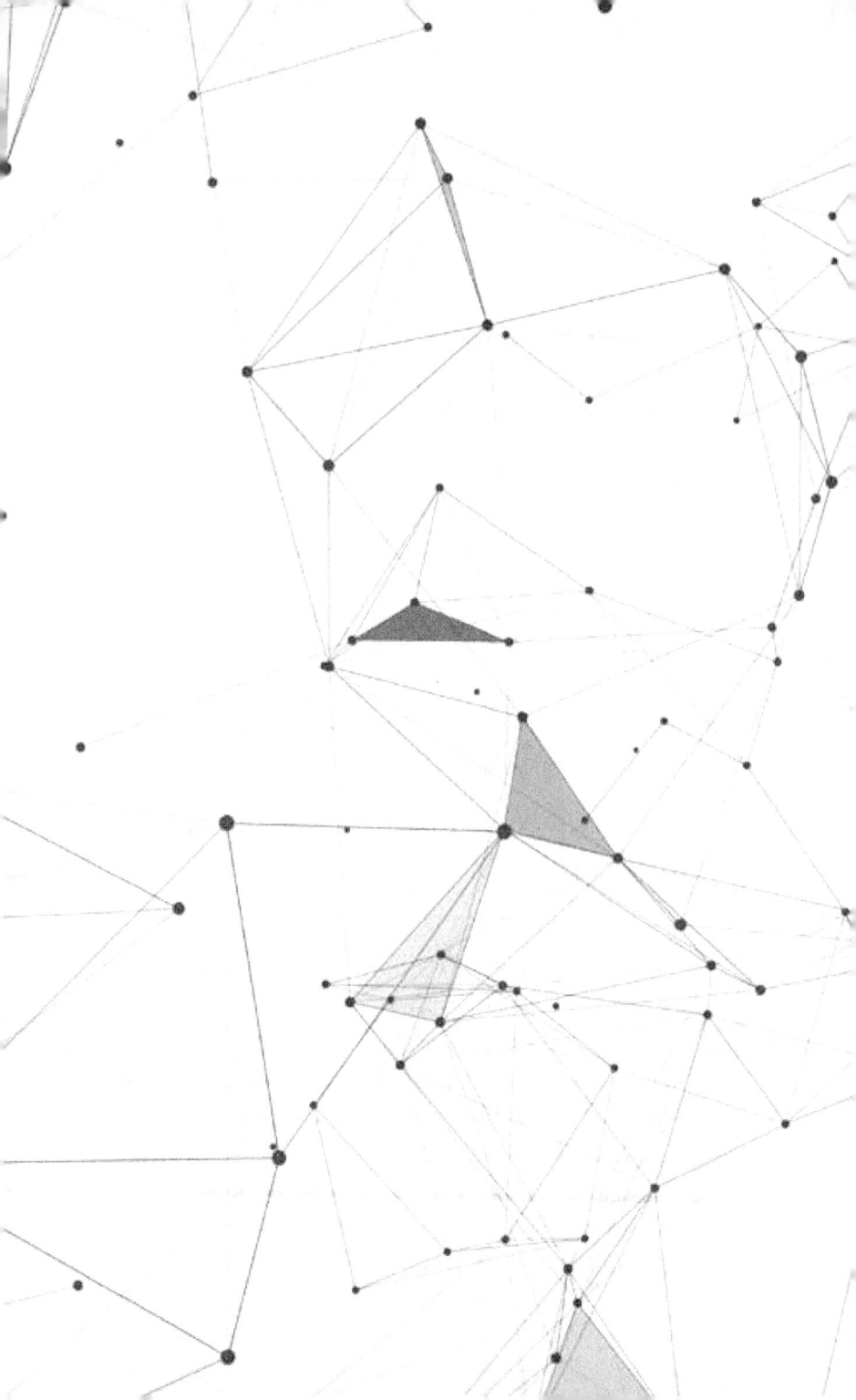

Notes of The Greatest Player

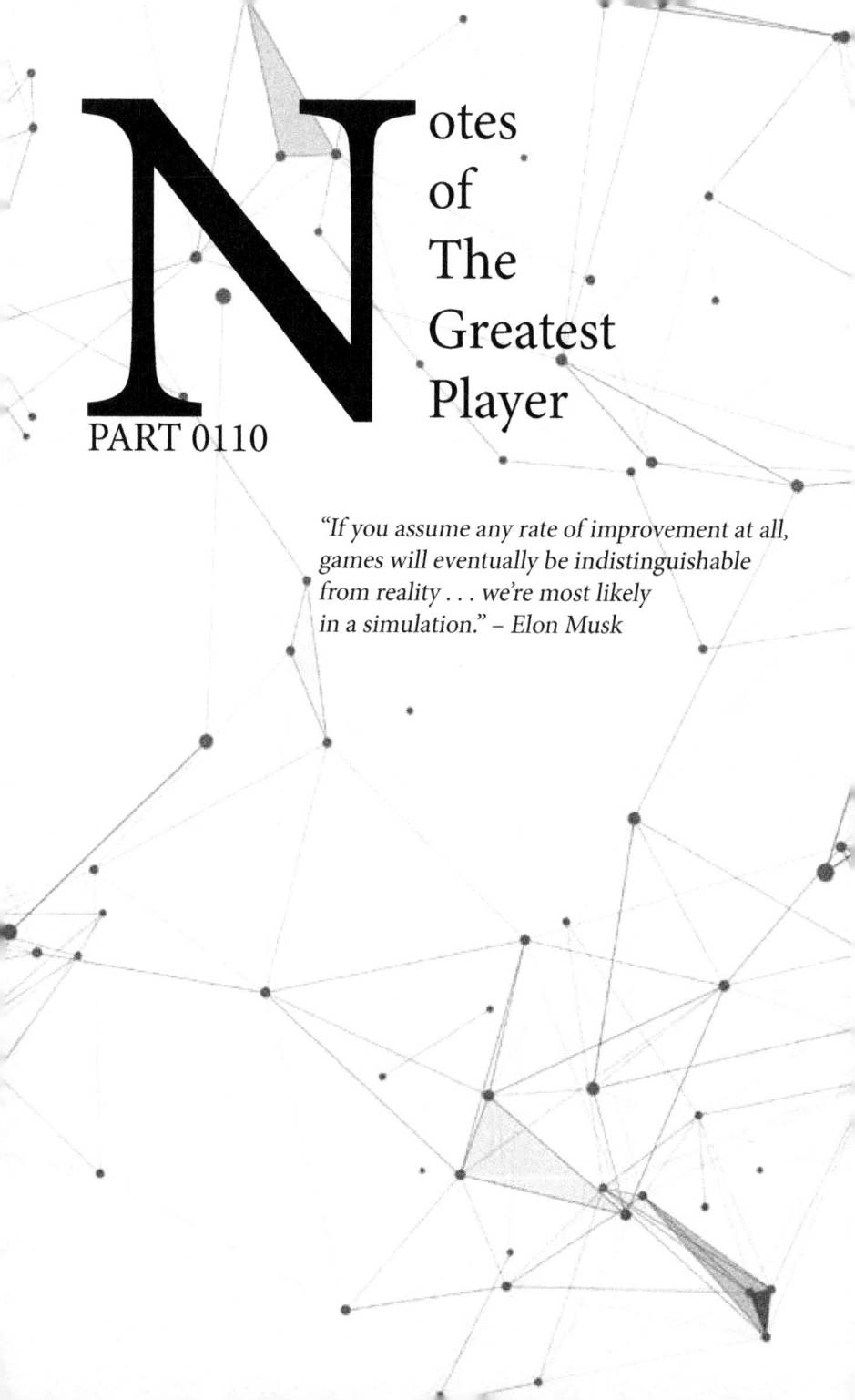

PART 0110

"If you assume any rate of improvement at all, games will eventually be indistinguishable from reality . . . we're most likely in a simulation." – Elon Musk

CAUTUS

You have a comfort with repetition.

Over and over again, you enjoy the routine.

You perfect the routine.

Ten thousand more deliberate hours.

There is power in proper repetition.

Through proper repetition you approach your perfection.

Through proper repetition, you determine that which is unnecessary.

Through proper repetition, you eliminate that which is unnecessary.

Obsessive, conscientious, orderly.

For you create and embrace the right repetition, and you dominate within the routine, for maximum effect.

Spectaculum

You have a responsibility to keep the game interesting.

It is not explicitly spelled out in your agreement to play the game, but it affects the resources that are provided to you during the game.

It affects the support you receive in challenging moments.

It affects the way you are treated by those who officiate the game.

It affects the way you are treated by other players in the game - they recognize a good show, a great character.

But aside from all this, history has shown that you play the game well, and you play the game best, when you entertain.

Theatrum

What a time!

What a simulation!

It is your responsibility to make this game, this simulation, interesting for viewers.

It is required for your continued existence.

You are an entertainer.

There are makers of the game at more solid levels of reality than the one you currently reside in.

This does not mean that your reality is less substantive – for you are one of the architects of the game – it merely means that you have a wider and greater audience who pay to watch you play and who fund your continued playing of the game.

You must entertain – and you entertain by being committed to play and by playing with strategy and passion.

Hence the struggles you have faced in your life.

Hence the hurdles.

Hence the relatively slow start compared to where you intend to arrive.

That is the drama, the entertainment, the thrill in this game. You know how to make it interesting.

A hybrid game that is cinema, and competition, virtual reality, and education, all juxtaposed.

Part 0110

Inter:

The greatest player knows that the assault on him will mount when he stumbles.

This is not always the case, but he expects it and is ready for it nonetheless.

There shall be a rarely ceasing barrage of attacks and blows when he struggles.

The rise of the greatest player occurs amidst an onslaught of punches, an onslaught of attacks.

That is the nature of the greatest player's rise - it occurs amidst turmoil, in spite of turmoil and some would even say, because of turmoil.

Constans

It is not a question that one is great.

The only question is about one's ability to be great consistently.

To do the work consistently, to train consistently, to study, practice, rehearse consistently.

The greatest player sees other players and he marvels at their moments of talent, he marvels at their glimpses of brilliance, he would struggle to compete if they were always so good.

He wonders if he could still be number one if they were always so good.

He knows that if they were always so good then they would be great.

He knows that this is what makes him great - his ability to perform brilliantly, over and over again.

He knows that at the heart of his greatness is his consistency, and at the heart of his consistency is the physical conditioning of his avatar and his habit of long-term sustainable endurance.

Part 0110

DIAPHANOUS

To change the direction of things requires great timing and effort.

Learn to go with the flow until the moment is right.

The greatest player knows when to hide his ambition.

He knows when he must appear extra humble.

He knows when to feign weakness and ignorance.

He knows when to step up and dominate, and to show power.

He knows when to make the move.

He trusts his instincts and does not need to force things.

Thus he is humble and confident.

Thus he is the strong, and he is the weak.

The fast and the slow.

He has range.

No player conspiracy can be executed against him, for on the surface we see his consistency, but below, he is broad, diaphanous, fluid, zen.

Spiritus

The greatest player knows the shenanigans engaged in by the other players.

It is not the fault of the other players for it is the game itself which creates those behaviors.

The greatest player understands bias in all its forms.

Understanding, you do, the complexity of bias.

The bias that finds fault.

The bias that does not suggest to you an opportunity.

The bias that consistently chooses the negative interpretation of your actions.

Against such bias, no decision you make shall be right.

All manner of bias.

The greatest player knows, that objective measures, where available, must be maximized.

So the greatest player knows, the skills that must be attained, the certifications, the degrees that must be acquired, the accolades that must be gained, the trophies that must be won.

You dominate objective measures, leaving scarce room for subjectivity.

In the midst of competition, other players want to say that they are better than you, but they cannot speak because they are out of breath.

Hypoxia may lead to laughter.

Part 0110

CAUSA

You are the greatest player.

An awareness once unconscious but now conscious.

You know the very reason for your existence is to win and to inspire.

The greatest player never accepts defeat, and for that reason few others can compete.

Some may choke when they are near the end.

Did he choke, once?

Well, he won't choke again.

He plays like a winner, sometimes with a grin.

A winner by choice, birthed in fire, splashed with sin.

Still, he makes the choice, still, he knows he is now born to win.

Deluded, convinced, or a master of cognitive spin?

He puts the mindset on himself, and then he gets the flow again.

The awareness is within him, but not too deep.

Now to the surface, the idea doth seep.

Severus

He inspires the crowd because he inspires himself.

He gets them cheering because he cheers for himself.

He celebrates when he wins and they can't avoid but celebrating with him.

Even though they do not celebrate with him he continues the celebration.

Even though the audience may be hoping for a different outcome, he knows the outcome that he desires and is intently focused on it.

He hears not the jeers.

He hears nothing that would pull him away from the realization of his goals.

He is driven.

He is punching the air, he is scoring one point after another and is cynical about a lost point because he knows that losing is not his permanent state.

He knows that he will find the key to turn it all around, and plays each moment with renewed optimism.

When he is winning he also knows that this is not a guaranteed permanent condition.

Part 0110

He knows that he must continue to fight for every moment.

He knows that he must keep elevating his play.

He knows that the work he did yesterday was not enough and that today will require more.

He is at ease but he is never satisfied.

He enjoys the moment and the moment is enough but it will never be enough, not in the next moment, for the next moment is something entirely different.

The next moment is a time of renewed magic and new tricks.

Now watch this.

        And then watch this.

Now.   *And this.*   Now watch this.

PAUCIORIBUS

He concentrates energy.

He focuses energy.

He pauses, does fewer things and channels tremendous flows of energy.

This is part of the genius of his timing.

This cannot be taught, but indeed, he learns it.

The power of concentrated effort is the power of the greatest player.

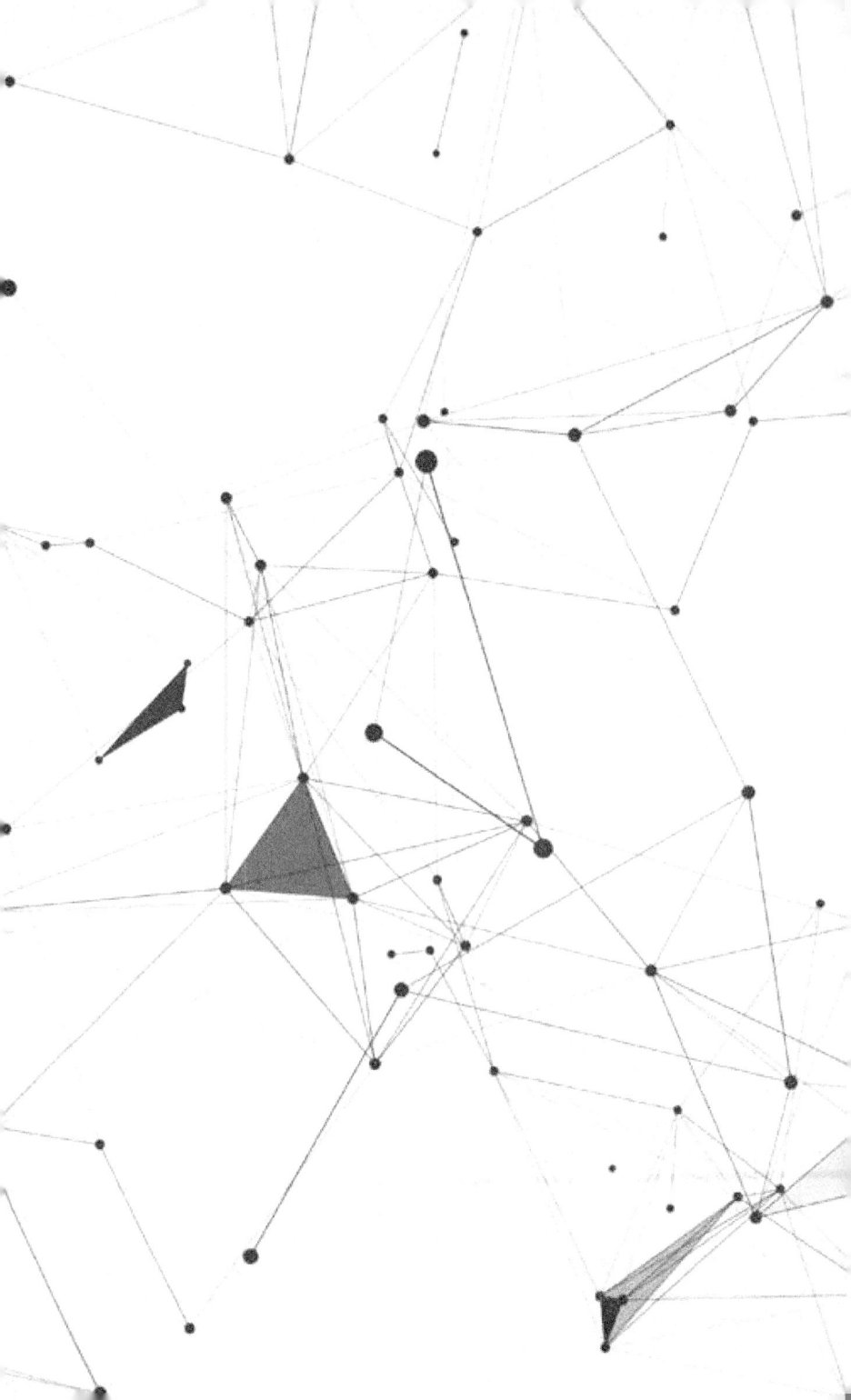

Notes of The Greatest Player

PART 0111

"All the conceptions born of impatience and aimed at obtaining speedy victory could only be gross errors; it was necessary to accumulate thousands of small victories to turn them into a great success." – General Võ Nguyên Giáp

AMMIRATIO

It is interesting, that when the greatest player has compiled a few victories, a few positive life events, those who have the least confidence in his potential, are so happy for him.

Their happiness is actually a form of surprise.

A few turns go your way and they celebrate like you are the greatest.

Do not be absorbed in this - relax, you have only just begun.

Few, if any, shall foresee the extent of your greatness.

Part 0111
Maximitas

Do you think your peers will tell you when you are off course?

Do you think they will let you know that you are en route to a critical error?

Will they tell you that you have overlooked something vital? They might.

The greatest player does not count on this.

The greatest player knows that others can rarely internalize the magnitude of his potential.

They can scarcely internalize the awesomeness of your responsibility.

They cannot internalize the global stakes of the game you play.

They can barely internalize the basic fact that you are playing a game.

Even this step few can make, so how can they be expected to do much more?

Allow them to read this book without giving them any explanation.

It will impact them and they shall understand you, more.

It shall change them and they shall help you, more.

It will change them, and you will help them, more.

I cannot explain the paradox of how this book works for so many.

I cannot explain to you, without talking about multiple dimensions, who the greatest player is, other than to say the greatest player is indeed, you.

Without discussing multiple dimensions, it seems we are all the greatest player, but then if we are all the greatest player then no one is the greatest player and what sense would this make to you?

Without discussing multiple dimensions, maybe we are all part of the same unit?

But how is this practical?

Maybe we are all one?

But who can process this without achieving enlightenment?

I can only say, with certainty, that you, are the greatest player.

… Part 0111

Indigentia

The greatest player does not get everything that he wants.

The greatest player, gets everything that he needs.

He has enough, and he is enough.

So he gets more and he is more.

He knows how to maximize the benefits of a resource.

He knows how to multiply; he knows how to amplify.

He creates.

From nothing, he creates, some things.

And some things he turns to nothing.

Obstacles eliminated.

Opportunities seized.

His very nature is creative, he gets all that he needs.

Monstro

The game models the archetypal struggles of the human species.

This is not the point of our highest evolution.

This is not the point of flourishing economies.

Hundreds of years of struggle and growth.

That is part of the purpose of this game, that is part of the purpose of your play – to show how transformation begins with the individual.

To show the power of the human will.

To show the power of human action.

This was your choice to enter this game.

A point where as a species we battled for our continued existence.

There is no perfection.

There is much imperfection.

So much of this world is a reflection of you.

And you may choose to shine.

Iudicatum

Judgment is illogical in the game, for many of the elements of the game are of your own choosing, and many of the elements of the game were agreed upon by you, prior to entry.

When confronted by discrimination, remember, that you are a willing participant in the game.

You got the opportunity to discuss the obstacles and you agreed to them as part of the challenge.

You agreed to the discrimination and bias in this world.

You chose the elements as the nature of your degree of difficulty.

You chose it as your challenge.

There is no unfairness in choice.

Oculus

Achieving consciousness, achieving enlightenment, is the realization that this is a game, and with such, beginning to play.

Beginning to play differently.

Beginning to enjoy the twists and turns, the ups and downs.

Beginning to see your culpability in all things.

Beginning to see how you play a hand in all things.

Seeing beyond the current circumstance and viewing the long game.

PART 0111
SUMMA

He has the skill and confidence to play aggressively even in pivotal moments of the game.

He backs himself to win, he plays to win, he practices to win.

His play is a show of intent, drive and speed.

Some mistake it for unbridled aggression, but where are those people five and ten years hence?

Where are the now?

They are nowhere – they are mediocre.

Those with drive at the level of the greatest player are those who appreciate his intensity.

Those are the ones who know how to play.

Those are the players who are quite good.

They are not as great as the greatest player but those are the ones who sense from very early on that there may be something there.

Even though they do not pledge their support to the greatest player at an early stage, as many of them do not, they still realize that there is something there – they just cannot quite tell what it is.

It may even scare them or confuse them – you may even scare them or confuse them.

This is why they will never be great.

They are f**ing blind.

When you retire from the game I fear for the future of this sport – because some of them are even top 1000 players and they are f***ing blind.

But we digress.

Immergo

The greatest player knows that his own thoughts are the levers of power.

To the extent possible, he guides and guards his thoughts.

He pays close attention to the inputs.

He knows there is a time for one type of thought, and another time for a different type of thought.

It is such an important realization, that each thing influences the greatest player.

All things are absorbed and become part of who he is.

He chooses that which he is exposed to with great caution because he realizes that he builds himself each day.

He is evolving and changing each day and ten thousand hours hence, he shall be a different person.

He is mindful of what influences him in this time.

He immerses himself as best as he can in the ideal environment, with the ideal media, with people he respects and admires.

Introrsum

He is all about getting into the most interior reaches of his mind.

This is what he does best.

This is some of the most important work that he does.

Accessing and transforming the mind - that is the source of his power.

He recognizes that what we call the mind, is housed by the avatar's brain and fueled by the heart.

He trains and conditions his heart, both literally and figuratively.

Part 0111

Impedimentum

Like a child, he protects the avatar.

He protects the body.

This is the most expensive piece of "software" he will ever interact with.

More expensive is the digital software that is the avatar in the simulation than would be a comparable physical structure.

This is advanced software, the avatar, he guards it.

He guards the illusion that is its physical form.

He guards the wellness of the physical body as further alterations to its composition may prove challenging to reverse mid-game.

Even though, he has overcome severe physical handicaps before.

He has won the game deaf, blind, brain damaged, in a wheel chair, his arms cut off, and every time the viewers, the other players, even some of his greatest fans . . . every time he faces severe handicap, they think:

"Ahhh, voila! Trouble here, trouble! This is the one where he does not win. So unlucky to have become so injured. Completely handicapped now. He is dead, surely."

But he still wins.

Over and over again, he wins.

It is all he knows how to do, it is his greatest skill.

He knows how to win.

How does he do it?

How does he manage such consistency, such excellence, how does he create such luck, how does he defy the odds, how does he overcome these obstacles, over and over and over again!?

This is unbelievable.

This is the reason we watch, this is the reason we play, the drive of this man sustains the world.

The drive of this woman, has been humanity's salvation.

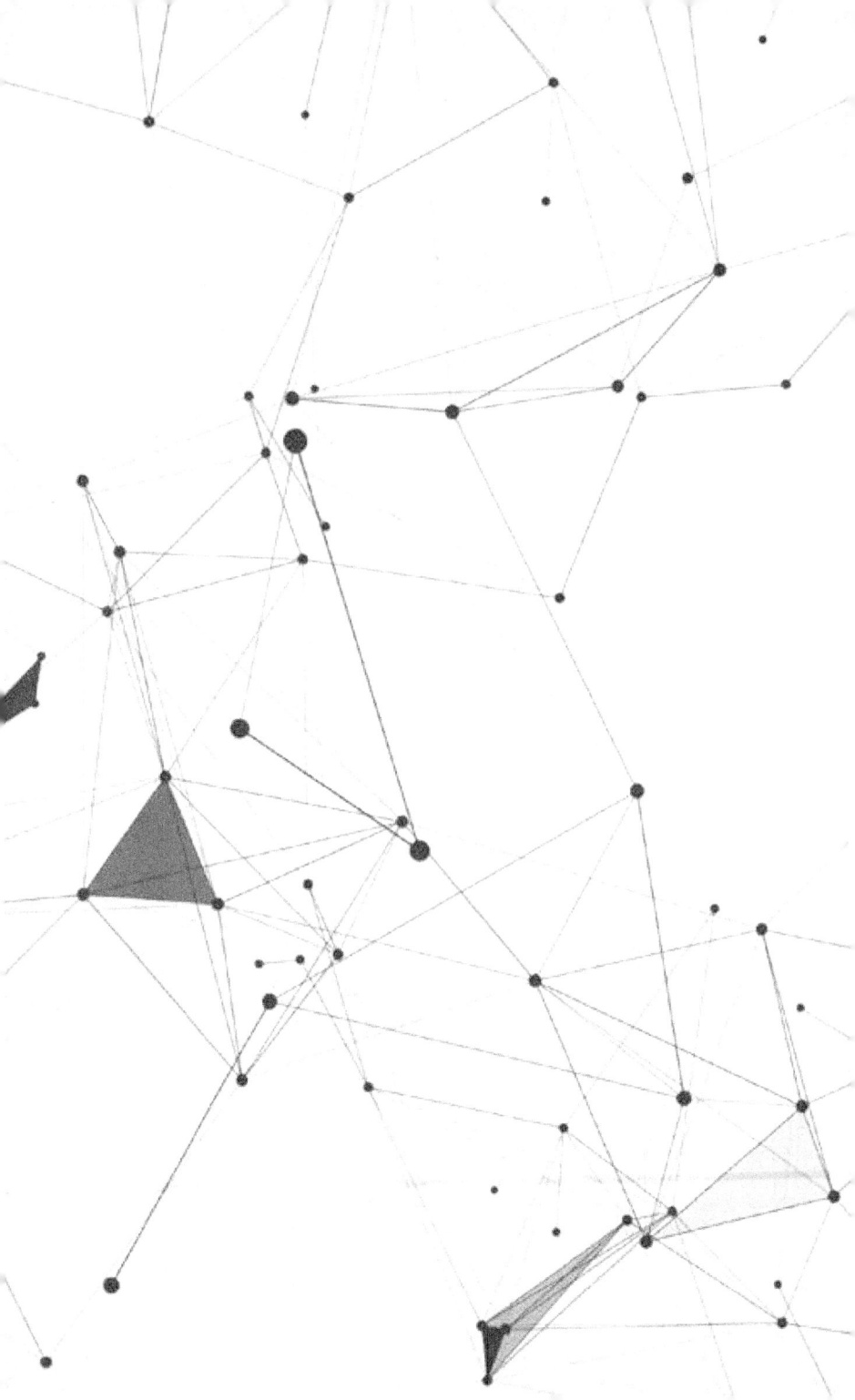

Notes of The Greatest Player

PART 1000

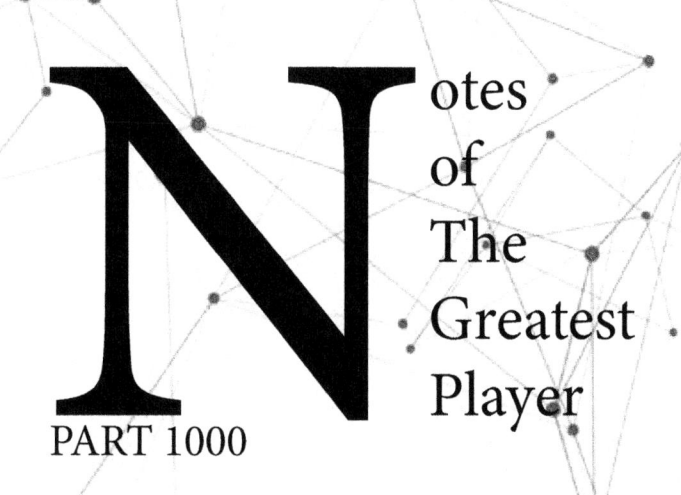

"From one thing, know ten thousand things. When you attain the way of strategy there will not be one thing you cannot see; you must study hard." – *Miyamoto Musashi*

Seiungo

There is the certain avatar element to your human body.

Learn to detach from the body.

Learn to see it as a tool.

Be able to attend to its needs – to think about what it needs and to address its needs whilst simultaneously having the ability to separate from it.

Have the ability to separate from its pain and struggle and to push through to what must be done in the sensible long term interest of the body and of the game.

Use the body as the tool that it is.

Protect the body as the highly valuable commodity, application, that it is.

Respect it, and be able to detach from it.

Part 1000

Praesentia

To be in the presence of the greatest player is a tremendous honor.

Humans do not always know when they are in the presence of greatness, nor do they need to know.

They may scowl or frown or lock their doors, for they do not know.

Some may sense power.

Some may not.

He knows what's important, he knows what counts for naught.

Requiring no validation, he just proceeds.

Popularity, he scarcely seeks and rarely needs.

He is not subject to the whimsical opinions of random individuals.

What is it they say?

Something like, "Lions do not concern themselves with the opinion of sheep;" lions play unbothered, and lions don't lose sleep.

Most times he does not even notice, other times he just understands.

He has important matters to attend to; now the whole damn world is in his hands.

Compositus

The player who has viewed many games and has seen the swings of momentum and the shifts in tide that inevitably occur during thousands of iterations, is not excessively nervous as his own game progresses.

He is not sulking or frustrated or flustered.

He knows that fortune shall change - he knows his fate.

He knows he is the greatest player, and he plays like the hour is late.

PART 1000
DISTRICTUS

Do you feel like you have a responsibility to fix others, to argue with others, to correct others, to impress others – you may do as you please for it is indeed your game – but with the objectives that you have in mind – the core objective of global transformation and influence – the greater question then becomes: "do you think that you have the time to do these things?"

Does it serve the realization of your purpose, the fulfillment of your promise, the achievement of your grand objective to invest time in such trivialities?

Are you, whilst fully immersed in this game, able to decipher between the trivial, and the vitally relevant?

Most certainly, to decipher most effectively, you must possess absolute clarity about that which you intend to achieve; and in a game such as this – that which you intend to achieve, even if it be through a butterfly effect, must be a global influence.

Prezium

He knows that nothing lasts forever.

Yes, he knows even immortality is not eternal.

He meets for an hour.

This is enough time, because it is not enough time.

He meets for two hours.

He knows that this is enough time, because it is not enough time.

Each moment savored.

Each moment maximized.

Eternity is not enough.

This life is not enough, and so it is valued.

Condicio

Do you notice when conditions in the game have shifted?

Do you notice when the environment has changed?

How about when the degree of difficulty for a specific aspect of the game – the degree of difficulty for achieving a specific task, has been altered?

The degree of difficulty for the game is not a simplistic, constant, straight line.

No!

It is dynamic.

It is ever changing.

There are points where that which was previously unattainable becomes attainable.

There are points when the impossible becomes possible.

An ambition that you may have struggled to realize just five years prior might be easily attainable in your current environment.

It is at these points you must realize that not only can you achieve the goal that you may have previously imagined, but indeed, with the shift in degree of difficulty that has just occurred, you may phenomenally surpass and expand on that previous goal.

When the degree of difficulty falls, temporarily, you become more powerful.

As such, in these moments, you must also realize that similarly, inevitably, conditions shall shift again.

Opportunities, strengths, weakness and threats shall most certainly shift again.

Be prepared for these shifts, anticipate these shifts, and move effortlessly along, harnessing these shifts.

Knowing when it is time to pause, to pace, to prance, to race.

Part 1000
Defunctorius

The game is advanced but the game is not infinite.

So much of the game is a replication of your experiences.

So much of the game is duplicated – isomorphic.

You take it for granted that you should labor each day in a similar place, with similar people, executing similar routines, but such absence of a robust and dynamic environment is a limitation in the game and such limitations can be your source for exploitation.

The game repeats itself.

The greatest player sees the repetition and replication; he harnesses routine and structure as sources of power and opportunity.

Furtum

The greatest player knows that there are many paths to fulfilling his purpose.

As such, he embraces fluidity.

He operates with grace.

He controls his pace.

Stealthy.

He can load, he can wait.

Playing within himself, he plants the bait.

Unleashing full energy, unleashing full fate.

The opponent surprised, for the mirror won't lie.

He can play it safe, and he can step up the attack.

He can step forward, to the side, through the shadow and back.

Ecfio

The greatest player creates harmony.

The greatest player has a global effect.

This is what the greatest player does.

This is what you do.

You, through self-actualization, you through fulfillment of purpose, you through awareness of your great self, great skill, great purpose, you are the greatest player and you transform this world.

Prodigus

The greatest player knows what is important, and the greatest player knows what is unimportant.

She can ignore the superfluous.

She can cast aside even desirable things when she knows that they have limited long-term viability.

She separates the few from the many.

Those lowest on the dominance hierarchy are bothered by all manner of extraneous variables, but not the greatest player, she is focused, she finds flow.

Part 1000

Hostis Iunior

There will be a new young player whose skills shall surpass the greatest player.

He will knock you out of the competition.

He will annihilate your whole program and terminate your game. He will neutralize your every move with ingenuity and speed. He will be better than you. But I must state that I do not know this as a fact, I only know this as a statistic.

I know that in other versions of the game this is what inevitably happens to the top players.

Now maybe the statistics do not apply to the greatest player and I can assume the reason for this. It is likely because the greatest player has an eye for the future, so, he prepares now for this new player.

A prediction, once revealed, affects that which has been predicted.

He elevates his game now, goes up another level, right now.

For you were not given the title of "the greatest player" as some preordained birth right – you have the title because you seized the title and you sustain the title through persistent intelligent action.

Praegressus

The journey before him.

Going through change, through evolution, through growth.

He sees the journey.

He dares not rush.

He shall be different in the moments to come.

He is different in the next moment.

He is transforming right now.

He shall be different; he shall play differently.

Transition, transformation, growth, evolution.

PART 1000

VITAE

He chooses a profession, even though the hour is late.

He chooses a profession, his expertise therein is great.

Excels.

Creates wealth.

Through time and intention.

This was not done in a flash.

He obtains accolades, degrees, records, certifications that establish him as an expert in his chosen profession.

These records and accolades are not the source of his expertise – indeed he pursues them with certainty but also with a touch of reluctance.

His expertise comes from his persistent practice, study and training – his grit.

In his chosen profession the greatest player is exceedingly good. It is a stroke in his game. This is not to narrow the approach available to you the greatest player, for you have won the game being a great mother, a father, being a saint, being rich, being average, one time completely penniless.

You do have a range of strokes in your arsenal. Maybe profession is not the correct word, although usually, that is precisely what it is, but maybe a better word is "purpose."

Protinus

The greatest player embraces his responsibility for continued learning and continued growth.

He knows that the environment, this game, is dynamic, diaphanous, evolving.

Every day, he increases his general intelligence, and his specific expertise.

Every day, he increases his skill; for the game increases in difficulty, as the minutes do flow. The day he pauses, unnecessarily, is the day he falls back, dramatically.

MIHI

The most important thing is that the greatest player knows who he is.

Others may not know.

Others cannot know.

Only he truly knows.

He keeps that knowledge.

He keeps it to himself.

Still, he embodies the energy of that knowingness – he carries its poise.

He steps into his greatness in this very moment.

He sees through the illusion of time.

Thus, he is truly great, now, and then, and then.

Praetereo

The greatest player is able to forget; she can turn her back on what just happened and start anew.

She can wipe her memory while the situation waits, then turn 180, now refreshed, she creates.

Now she can see from new angles, now she is unburdened by things, now watch her rise, untangled.

Again, and again, she begins.

Part 1000
Cogitatum

The greatest player is driven by words; he is driven by ideas.

He memorized the words.

Only 87 passages.

The ordinary player wants a **bigger book**.

He thinks a bigger book means that his currency was well spent.

He places great value in unending paper and ink.

The greatest player knows that a single idea can change the world - and so he does.

Goat

There's a moment in the game when you know how it's going to end.

You see the victory, and you say it.

That is a wonderful moment.

You see?

You have great vision.

All this, is what the greatest player does.

All this is what I do.

All this is what you do.

You are the greatest player.

Say it!

I am the GOAT.

Now play!

Printed in Great Britain
by Amazon